D1738866

PRESCRIPTION DRUG ABUSE

Abusing prescription medication can be extremely dangerous.

THE DRUG ABUSE PREVENTION LIBRARY

PRESCRIPTION DRUG ABUSE

Jeremy Roberts

The Rosen Publishing Group, Inc.
New York

The people pictured in this book are only models. They in no way practice or endorse the activities illustrated. Captions serve only to explain the subjects of photographs and do not in any way imply a connection between the real-life models and the staged situations.

Published in 2000 by The Rosen Publishing Group, Inc.
29 East 21st Street, New York, NY 10010

First Edition

Library of Congress Cataloging-in-Publication Data

Roberts, Jeremy
   Prescription drug abuse / by Jeremy Roberts.
     p. cm. — (The drug abuse prevention library)
   Includes bibliographical references and index.
   Summary: Discusses how prescription drugs are abused, how to recognize this problem in parents and friends, and how to seek help.
   ISBN 0-8239-3158-7 (lib. bdg.)
   1. Drug abuse—Juvenile literature. 2. Substance abuse—Physiological aspects—Juvenile literature. [1. Drugs. 2. Drug abuse.] I. Title. II. Series.
   RC564.3 .R63 2000
   362.29'9—dc21
                             99-048023
                                   CIP
                                   AC

Manufactured in the United States of America

Contents

	Introduction	6
Chapter 1	Mother's Little Helper	10
Chapter 2	What's an Rx, Anyway?	14
Chapter 3	Commonly Abused Drugs	21
Chapter 4	Steroids	35
Chapter 5	Abusing Prescription Drugs	41
Chapter 6	Reactions and Interactions	46
Chapter 7	How Do You Tell Someone . . .	51
	Glossary	57
	Where to Go for Help	59
	For Further Reading	61
	Index	62

Introduction

Jen rubbed her face and glanced toward the front of the classroom. Her math teacher, Mr. Phillips, was explaining how to solve a geometry problem. Math was one of her best subjects, but suddenly nothing Mr. Phillips was saying made sense. In fact, it sounded to Jen as if he were speaking a foreign language.

Actually, she wasn't thinking much about anything. She did, however, feel incredibly tired. She closed her eyes and felt herself falling right into bed. Except that it wasn't her bed she was falling toward; it was the floor.

The next thing Jen knew, she was in the school nurse's office. The nurse was there, along with the vice principal. They kept asking her questions. The questions were harsh. They wanted to know why she'd fallen asleep. One of her friends had apparently told the vice

An inability to concentrate is one of the first signs of prescription drug abuse.

principal that she had seen Jen take some pink pills. They wanted to know what they were.

Jen shrugged. She felt very far away, as if she were lying at the bottom of a ten-foot-deep pool. They wanted her to wake up. The nurse, normally a calm little old lady, was screaming at her. Jen tried to tell her that there wasn't a problem. She was just tired, that's all.

Then an ambulance attendant came into the room. More questions. What did she take? Jen tried to tell them that she had taken two pills. They were prescription drugs that her friend Kristen had given her. It was a prescription that Kristen's mom had gotten some time ago—painkillers or something. Jen had even taken one once before. But she was so tired

8 | *that her mouth just didn't seem to work. She started slipping back into sleep . . .*

Every year, millions of people in America abuse prescription drugs. They do this in one of several ways. They may fail to follow the directions that come with the prescription and take incorrect dosages. They may take the drug when they don't need it. Or they may take prescription drugs that haven't been prescribed for them.

In some cases, a person takes too large a dose or combines the drug with another potentially dangerous substance, such as alcohol. In other cases, a person might start taking a prescription drug for a legitimate reason and then continue to take it long after the original medical problem goes away. To get more drugs, a person might pretend to be hurt or sick long after there is any real need for medication. Or perhaps he or she buys the drug from a friend.

Sometimes, as in Jen's case, a drug abuser has no idea what drug he or she is taking. Little or nothing is known about its side effects or how it may interact with other drugs. Some people call this recreational drug use. Others say it's just Russian roulette with pills.

In this book, you will learn about different kinds of prescription drugs and the health problems they may cause if taken incorrectly or taken when there is no reason to do so. You will learn about bad drug reactions and how to seek help for yourself or a friend in dealing with chemical dependency. And most of all, you will learn that just because prescription drugs are dispensed legally, they are not necessarily safe.

9

CHAPTER 1

Mother's Little Helper

*P*rescription drug abuse has been a problem for as long as there have been prescriptions. Certain drugs have a lengthy history of being abused. The abuse of "pep pills," or amphetamines, was so widespread when your grandparents were young, for example, that a famous rock group, the Rolling Stones, wrote a song about them called "Mother's Little Helper." The song made fun of the growing number of ordinary, respectable people who had come to depend on these pills to control their moods and deal with the stresses of life.

Not all prescription drugs are addictive, and not all of them have mind-altering effects. But nonaddictive prescription drugs still can cause problems, especially if their effects on the body are complicated, as they often are. Intimate knowledge of a

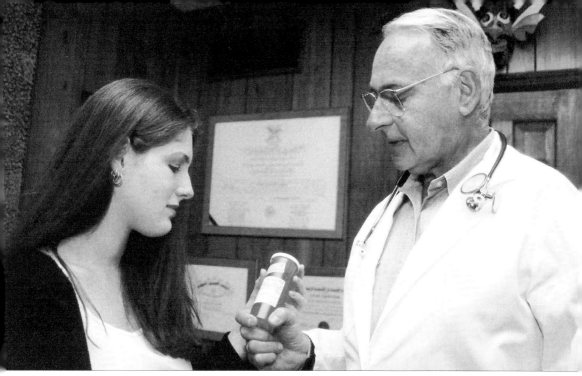

Prescription drug abuse is a serious problem with a long history.

person's previous health history is important in prescribing these types of drugs. The size and timing of dosages may be critically important. And some drugs can have dangerous side effects for a small percentage of people. These factors all must be weighed when prescribing such drugs. Simple precautions by the doctor and pharmacist may save a patient's life. Someone who abuses a prescription drug is ignoring these precautions and may pay for it with his or her life.

Taking a pill when you don't know what it is or where it came from is just plain stupid. Taking medicine that hasn't been prescribed for you can end your life.

12

Of course, the potential dangers of prescription drugs shouldn't frighten you to the point that you never take any medicine. But it is important to give doctors and pharmacists as much information as you can about allergies and reactions to other medicines that you may have had. You should also inform your doctor of any other medicines—either prescription or over-the-counter drugs—that you are taking. Don't be afraid to ask your doctor questions about a prescription drug and its side effects. And never take medicine that has been prescribed for someone else, even if you think you have the same illness.

What Happened to Jen

Jen took two pills of propoxyphene, a powerful pain reliever prescribed under the brand name Darvon. Ordinarily this pain-killer can alleviate suffering and is very useful when prescribed properly. But it can also cause death. According to the Federal Drug Administration (FDA), as many as 2,000 people a year die from improper doses of this drug.

Jen's story had a happy ending. The dose she took wasn't life threatening. She didn't stop breathing or have a seizure. She just fell asleep, right in the middle of math class. Unfortunately, the people trying to help her had no way of knowing that. In fact, Jen had no way of knowing that. She could easily have taken a much greater dose and experienced those same symptoms before things got worse.

Even though her life was not in danger, Jen ended up having her stomach pumped, which wasn't very pleasant. She also had to explain to her parents what had happened and was given detention at school. Her friend Kristen nearly was charged with a crime and taken to family court. Kristen was grounded for "the next nine lifetimes," in her father's words. But considering what could have happened, everyone involved was very lucky.

CHAPTER 2

What's an Rx, Anyway?

*T*he odds are that you started taking your first prescription medicine before you were born. That's because many women are given a prescription for special vitamins when they are pregnant. The vitamins include special substances that help the fetus to develop. And those vitamins are just the beginning. Even healthy mothers may use several medications during the course of a pregnancy.

Over-the-Counter Drugs
In the United States, we divide medicine into two categories: prescription drugs and over-the-counter drugs.

In general, over-the-counter drugs can be bought anywhere by anyone. They are usually common drugs that everyone knows about. Aspirin, cough medicine, and most of the antihistamines used for allergies and colds are good examples. Over-the-counter medicines include drugs that you swallow, such as aspirin. They also include drugs that you apply topically to your body, such as calamine lotion for skin rashes. One expert estimates that there are more than 300,000 over-the-counter drugs available, and new versions come out every day.

Sometimes, drugs start out as prescription drugs and then become over-the-counter drugs. Often, that happens to drugs after they have been used for many years. In most cases, medical authorities have come to understand that such drugs are not easily abused. Drugs that help to reduce stomach acid and relieve the effects of ulcers are good examples of drugs that began as prescription drugs and then became available over the counter.

Over-the-counter drugs are usually less expensive than are prescription drugs. They are certainly easier to obtain, since you don't have to see a doctor and you don't need a pharmacist to prepare them. But it's important to remember that over-the-counter drugs can be abused just as prescription drugs can. Even though they generally are not as strong or dangerous as

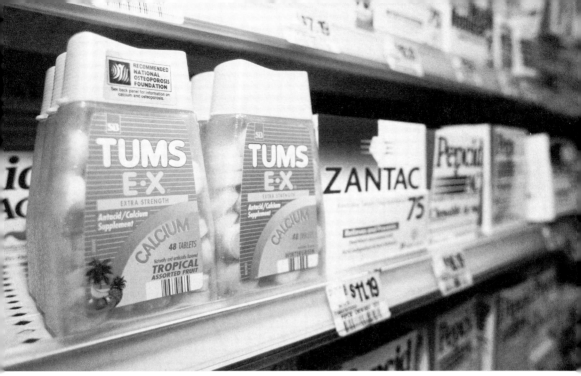

Seemingly harmless drugs can be dangerous when abused.

prescription medicines, they still can do harm under the wrong circumstances. For example, even a small dose of aspirin irritates some people's stomachs. Taking too many aspirin tablets can cause bleeding. That's why it's always important to follow carefully the directions on all medicines.

By Prescription Only

In general, prescription medicines are stronger and more dangerous than are over-the-counter drugs, if used incorrectly. In most cases, a doctor must personally examine a patient and conclude that a particular drug will help before writing the prescription. The prescription for the drug is then given to a licensed pharmacist, who

makes sure that the right drug and the | *17*
proper dosage are prepared. Ultimately, of
course, it is up to the patient to take the
medicine correctly. Prescription drugs are
controlled by federal and state laws. These
laws dictate how such drugs can be prescribed and used.

A drug's potential to be abused or to
cause addiction is one reason why it may
be available only by prescription. But it's
not the only reason. Not all prescription
drugs are addictive. They may have very
strong side effects or cause serious problems for some people when used incorrectly. Powerful medicines, such as
antibiotics, must be chosen carefully to do
the most good. In some cases, a drug may
be so new that doctors are still learning
how best to use it.

In all of these cases, the prescription system allows doctors and other health care
workers to keep an eye on things. The
system is designed to protect patients, who
may not have detailed knowledge about a
drug or who may be vulnerable to the medicine's side effects.

Unfortunately, in a small percentage of
instances, doctors and pharmacists are part
of the problem. For example, some doctors
may write prescriptions even though they

Prescription drugs that have a high potential for being abused are carefully regulated by both the government and pharmacists.

know or suspect that the medicine will be abused. Or they won't check a patient as carefully as they might to make sure that a certain drug really is needed.

Prescription drugs that have a high potential for being abused are under special regulation by the federal government. They often are called controlled substances. The federal drug regulations have different lists, or schedules, of drugs. Schedule I drugs, which include illegal substances such as heroin, generally have no medical use and are rarely, if ever, prescribed.

Schedule II drugs do have legitimate medical uses, but they can be easily abused and may be addictive. Using them improperly can be catastrophic. Some examples are morphine and amphetamines. Schedule II drugs, once prescribed, cannot be refilled except by going to the doctor and getting a new prescription. Schedule III and IV drugs are less addictive and dangerous, though they, too, can be abused. Refills of these drugs are limited.

You or someone you know probably has had a schedule II or a schedule III drug. Empirin with codeine, for example, often is given after oral surgery. This combination of codeine and aspirin is a very effective painkiller, if used correctly. Because it can be abused, however, it is a schedule III drug.

Pharmacists receive extensive training in many aspects of drug therapy. They must work hard to keep themselves up-to-date in their field, which is rapidly changing. One of the most important things pharmacists do is to check on the ways in which different drugs interact. These interactions can be quite confusing and many pharmacies use computers to help them watch for potential problems.

In the old days, pharmacists often mixed the chemicals for certain drugs themselves. In Great Britain, they're still

Pharmacists are highly trained in chemistry and medicine.

called chemists. Although today's pharmacists do know a great deal about chemistry, most drugs come from their manufacturers in prepared form in large batches, which must be individually packaged by pharmacists and their assistants. Pharmacists find that they must know a lot more than just chemistry to master their science. Just sorting out some of the long names of medicines, which often sound similar, can be a challenge.

CHAPTER 3

Commonly Abused Drugs

*T*he dentist gave Bill a shake of his head. "I'm afraid that tooth is going to have to come out," he said.

"Will it hurt?" asked Bill. His mouth ached so badly that the words slurred together and he practically choked getting them out.

"Well, it won't hurt as much in the long run if we take care of it now," said the dentist. "We can dull the pain during the surgery with Novocain and laughing gas. And I'll give you a prescription for some Empirin with codeine. That will make it feel better."

Bill was dubious. But sure enough, the Novocain and laughing gas dulled the pain. His head felt very light. His sister had come with him to the dentist. They stopped at the drugstore on the way home. The pharmacist explained

22 *that Empirin with codeine was a combination of aspirin and codeine. Aspirin helped to relieve pain and inflammation, or swelling. Codeine was a pain reliever. The two drugs worked very well together, the pharmacist explained.*

Bill agreed, especially when he felt better shortly after he took his prescribed pill. In fact, he thought he felt calmer and more at ease when he took the drug. He certainly slept very well.

On Thursday, he took his last pill. Though he no longer felt any pain, Bill thought about calling the dentist and asking for more pills.

"They made me feel more relaxed," he explained. "But then I read the paper that the pharmacist gave me. It told all about the drug. There were all sorts of possible side effects. Then I saw that it could be addictive. I didn't want to mess with it."

Painkillers: Opiates and Opioids

Many of the most commonly abused drugs are those used to help deal with pain. These drugs are of vital importance to many people. They make surgery possible. They help people to overcome difficult physical and mental problems. But they also can be very dangerous, especially when they are abused. And some can be very tempting.

Bill's combination drug is a very common

All prescription medications should only be used according to your doctor's instructions.

prescription. It can be very effective against pain and often is prescribed following surgery. Its potential to cause addiction or generate unpleasant side effects is actually very low, especially compared to other drugs in the opiate/opioid family, which includes codeine. Drugs belonging to the opiate/opioid family are also known as narcotic analgesics or simply narcotics. All are related chemically to opium, which comes from poppies and has a long history as an addictive drug. The drugs are divided into two groups, according to how they are made. Opioids are made synthetically in the laboratory. Opiates come from nature, that is, from the juice of the poppy plant.

24   Other drugs in this family include Percodan and Demerol. These powerful painkillers often are used in hospitals. Another member of this drug family is heroin, which illustrates how dangerous these drugs can be. An extremely addictive and destructive drug, heroin is the most infamous member of the opiate family. Some opiates are stronger than others, but when used improperly, all members of this drug family can be habit-forming.

     Opiates and opioids generally give patients a dreamy kind of rush. Then users sink into a kind of gentle oblivion, in which they cannot feel much pain—just the sort of thing you need when you're undergoing an operation. In general, these drugs slow breathing and other bodily functions. The effects of such drugs can be magnified if combined with another depressant, such as alcohol.

     An overdose of opiates or opioids can be lethal. This is a serious problem because users build up tolerances to these drugs quickly. Over time, it takes more and more of the drug to produce the same pain relief or rush. Users rapidly reach the point where they are taking dangerously high doses. Unfortunately, this makes it hard to use opiates or opioids as painkillers for long periods of time.

The most commonly abused members of the opiate/opioid drug family include hydrocodone and codeine, which are often combined with analgesics. Analgesics are drugs that produce pain relief without unconsciousness. Hydrocodone combinations rank among the most prescribed drugs in the country. Common brand names include Vicodin and Lortab. Darvon, another painkiller that is chemically related to methadone, is among the top twenty abused drugs, according to the Drug Enforcement Administration (DEA).

Sedatives

Opiates often are prescribed to relieve pain during or after surgery. Sedatives are also used during surgery for a similar purpose. Basically, sedatives make you go to sleep. These drugs sedate, or render a patient unconscious, so that he or she doesn't feel anything during an operation. Sedatives are also prescribed to relieve anxiety or reduce the possibility of epileptic seizures. Someone who takes a sedative may feel happy at first and then get so tired that he or she falls asleep. In some

Sedatives are often derived from the poppy plant.

26 | ways, the effects of alcohol and sedatives are very similar.

There are several different types of sedatives. The barbiturates make up the largest family of sedatives. This family of drugs gets its name from barbital, which was invented in 1903. All barbiturates are man-made. Some examples of barbiturates are Nembutal, Seconal, and Tuinal. Barbiturates used to be prescribed for anxiety disorders and sleeplessness, but because they are so addictive, their use for these types of problems has stopped.

Methaqualone, also known as quaalude, is a nonbarbiturate sedative once thought to be free from the dangerous side effects of barbiturates. Unfortunately, that did not prove to be the case. "Ludes" became a widely abused drug during the 1960s and 1970s. Not only is the drug highly addictive, but someone who stops taking it risks a serious epileptic seizure. Methaqualone is no longer manufactured in the United States, but pills are available illegally from other countries.

GHB, or gamma-hydroxybutyrate, is a sedative that is used for general anesthesia in Europe but not ordinarily in the United States. It is sometimes illegally synthesized as a liquid drink in home labs and was once

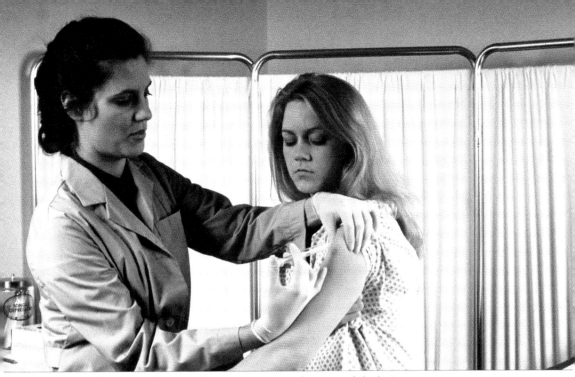
Sedatives and tranquilizers are extremely powerful; their use must be monitored by medical professionals.

available over the counter. Bodybuilders sometimes used it to help during training. Sales of GHB now are illegal in the United States. Drug experts are not yet sure exactly how GHB works, but its effects include nausea and loss of consciousness. It also can lead to coma and death. It is one of the "date rape" drugs, used to render a rape victim unconscious and unable to offer testimony against her attacker.

Tranquilizers

Tranquilizers reduce tension and anxiety and promote a relaxed, calm mental state. Tranquilizers can be broken down into two categories: major tranquilizers, which

28 are used for psychotic states such as schizophrenia; and minor tranquilizers, which are intended to calm anxiety.

Major tranquilizers are not commonly abused for a number of reasons. They are, however, extremely powerful drugs that can have serious side effects, even when used properly. Minor tranquilizers are safer than drugs such as barbiturates. But they, too, can be abused.

One of the best-known minor tranquilizers is Valium. It belongs to a family of drugs called benzodiazepines. Other drugs in this family include Ativan, Dalmane, Halcion, Serax and Xanax. These drugs depress the body's natural reactions, such as fear and nervousness. When used in combination with psychological counseling, they are effective weapons against anxiety disorders. In some situations, they can help patients who need to get sleep or who need to recover from traumatic situations.

But Valium and its kin also can be easily abused. One expert estimated that in the late 1980s as many as 11 percent of all Americans used tranquilizers. That high a number, he said, indicated that the drug was being prescribed much too frequently.

One member of the benzodiazepine

The drug Rohypnol is tasteless and colorless, and it can be used to render potential date rape victims unconscious.

family that recently has gained a very bad reputation is Rohypnol, known on the street as "roofies." This is another date rape drug; some men have used the drug to render women unconscious and rape them. It can easily be added to drinks. Because the drug acts as a sedative, someone taking it may pass out or become much more open to suggestion than under normal circumstances.

Minor tranquilizers, when used incorrectly, can cause chemical dependence or addiction. Their effects also can be multiplied by alcohol and other drugs. Although tranquilizers are in some ways safer than depressants, doctors now realize that tranquilizers can be easily abused.

Antidepressants

Psychiatrists and psychologists use powerful drugs to help people with clinical depression. Sometimes called mood elevators, there are a number of important antidepressants. Used with counseling, these drugs can help patients to cope with mental illnesses that might otherwise lead to suicide.

In general, antidepressants take a long time to work. Their effects are measured in days and weeks, not minutes. That makes them unlikely candidates for abuse. As with any other medicine, however, they can be misused. And their abuse can be very serious.

One of the biggest families of antidepressants is the group of drugs called tricyclic antidepressants. They all are mild sedatives. Overdosing can cause a range of symptoms, from confusion to heart failure. The effects of these drugs are multiplied by alcohol.

Researchers are working to find other drugs that can act as safe antidepressants. Prozac, which is not a tricyclic, wasn't even included in some books on common drugs a decade ago. Now it rates among the most prescribed medicines in the country. But it, too, can cause severe health problems if abused or used with other medicines.

Stimulants

Stimulants range from caffeine, which is an important ingredient in coffee and some sodas, to cocaine and methamphetamine. Caffeine, at least in the amounts found in coffee and soda, generally is considered harmless. Some studies have raised questions about consuming large amounts of caffeine, however. Many doctors now recommend moderation. Caffeine pills, which generally contain about the same caffeine as a cup or two of strong coffee, are available as over-the-counter drugs.

The most important family of medical stimulants is the amphetamine group. In general, these drugs speed up the body's activities. Taking one is like feeding a steady stream of adrenaline into the bloodstream.

The legitimate uses of stimulants include fighting illnesses such as attention deficit disorder (ADD) and narcolepsy. Stimulants also are sometimes prescribed as appetite suppressants to help people lose weight. This practice has been strongly criticized by the FDA.

The potential side effects of amphetamines include an irregular heartbeat, liver damage, and cerebral hemorrhage. Regular abusers of these pills, which are also known

Some teens drink cold medicines to get high because many contain alcohol and other depressants.

as "uppers," "greens," or "pep pills," can develop mental disorders.

Methylphenidate hydrochloride, better known as Ritalin, is another stimulant. Ritalin has become a very important drug over the past decade because of its use in treating ADD. Even though it is a stimulant and patients with ADD are hyperactive, the drug counteracts that hyperactivity. Instead of speeding up nervous activity, Ritalin slows it down. Ritalin usually acts as a stimulant for people without ADD. After the initial rush, however, the body tends to crash sharply, that is, sink into a deep state of depression.

Unfortunately, the fact that the drug is widely available for ADD has made it

easier to abuse. In some cases, patients | *33*
have given their prescription pills to
friends. In other cases, the drug has been
stolen or illegally obtained.

Robo Shots
Prescription medicines aren't the only
drugs that are abused, of course. Over-
the-counter drugs also can be used incorrectly to get high or enhance the effects of
other substances.

Among the most frequently abused over-
the-counter medicines, especially in middle
schools, are liquid cough and cold medicines. Drinking large quantities of cough
and cold medicines is sometimes called
"doing Robo shots." The slang term comes
from Robitussin, the name of a popular
brand of cough medicines, but it is not the
only cough medicine that can be abused.

Many cough and cold remedies contain
mild depressants or alcohol. Strong night-
time cold medicines, for example, may include antihistamines, dextromethorphan (a
cough suppressant), and alcohol. All of
these can cause sleepiness in very high
doses. Some cold medicines also contain
pseudoephedrine, a nasal decongestant
that in high doses can cause dizziness and
nervousness.

34 Allergy medicines usually contain some form of antihistamine. Antihistamines block histamine, a chemical released by the body during allergic reactions. In layman's terms, they trick the body into not reacting to something to which it is allergic. Antihistamines dry up nasal passages in particular and the body in general. They also can make someone drowsy or even a little dopey. They can multiply the effects of alcohol and barbiturates.

It's important to remember that all of these medicines, from opiates to over-the-counter cold remedies, generally are beneficial when properly used. From the patient undergoing knee surgery to the hay fever sufferer, modern medicine plays an important role in improving everyone's quality of life. But all bets are off when medicines are abused or incorrectly used.

CHAPTER 4

Steroids

*T*he mirror doesn't lie. Your muscles just aren't getting any bigger. All of those extra laps and free weight repetitions just aren't paying off. No way you're going to be bulky enough when football season starts. At least that's what you were thinking before a buddy offered a solution—a bunch of steroids a friend of a friend got from Mexico off the Internet.

For fifty dollars, you can add five inches to your chest. The pills come with a brochure that says they're not steroids, but "precursors" to steroids. You carefully follow the instructions. You also continue to eat well and exercise like a demon. And guess what? You add not five inches, but nearly ten inches to your chest. You make

36 the team, but something nags at you from the back of your mind. Isn't all of this too good to be true?

Anabolic steroids and other physique enhancers are among the most controversial medicines being prescribed today. Anabolic steroids are chemically similar to testosterone, the male sex hormone. Testosterone has, on occasion, been used to artificially enhance sports performances. There are many other types of steroids besides anabolic steroids. Birth control pills, for example, are a type of steroid.

Some experts say that steroids don't do anything that the body isn't doing for itself. Others, including many athletes who have used them, point to bigger muscles and increased performance. Some draw a line between steroids that are illegal and "supplements" that are similar to steroids but not illegal.

The issue is a complicated one. Some substances, such as vitamins, clearly are beneficial nearly all of the time, and not just to athletes. New medicines appear all of the time, and even the experts can become confused. A host of substances are said to mimic steroids' benefits without the downsides. Others are called "presteroids" and are said to encourage the body to

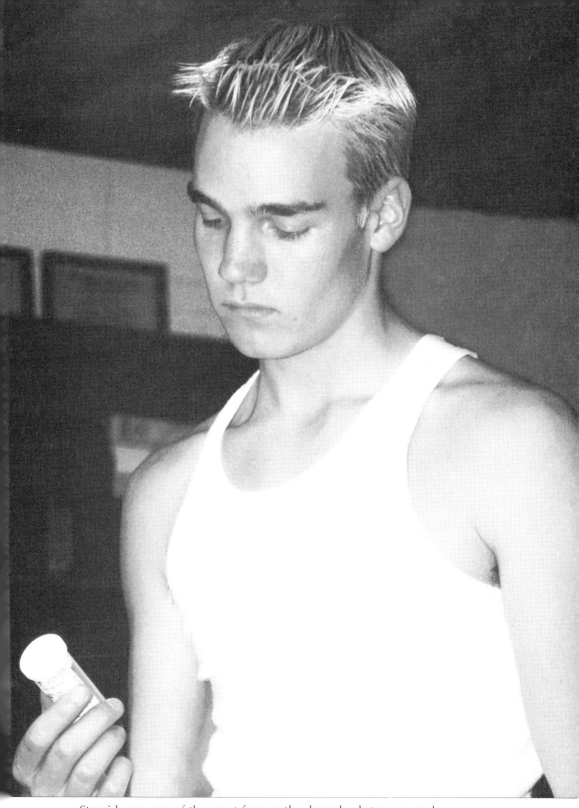

Steroids are one of the most frequently abused substances, and
one of the most dangerous.

38 | produce steroids on its own. It's often difficult to separate the facts from the boasts.

Mark McGwire one of the greatest home run hitters of all time, used a supplement known as andro (androstenedione) during the year he broke Roger Maris's home run record. He said that he used it because he wanted to recover from an injury. The substance was not illegal or banned in baseball, although other sports organizations did ban it.

After the controversy began, McGwire stopped using andro. But he still kept hitting monster home runs. Some people believe this is proof that such supplements don't work. Others disagree and say andro helped McGwire get back in shape after his injury. The debate most likely will continue for several years, as new discoveries are made and new claims for the supplements' health benefits are tested.

Steroids Are Out
Right now, though, most people recognize that steroids are extremely dangerous. Most sports conferences routinely test for steroids. Anyone who uses them is banned from competition. Although they're legally sold without prescriptions in Mexico, just having them in your

It is safest to improve muscles through proper diet and exercise.

pocket without a prescription is a federal offense in the United States.

Why should that be, though, if they build muscles? Isn't that the point of training in the first place? Anabolic steroids are believed to damage the liver. Some experts say that they cause cancer of the prostate and liver. They increase blood pressure, which can lead to a host of heart and circulatory system problems. They also can harm male reproductive organs and alter women's natural hormonal states. Steroids have been blamed for stimulating aggressive behavior, known as "roid rage."

According to the National Institute for Drug Abuse, teenagers can be more seriously harmed by steroids than can

42 | *drinking alcohol, which could have presented real problems.*

"We learned all about this in school," she admitted. "Alcohol is like a multiplier. It increases the effect of the drug. You could pass out. It could even cause a coma."

So why did she take the pill in the first place?

"I'm not really sure. I don't know if it was peer pressure or stupidity or what," she said. "It was just there, you know. So, like, everybody else was doing it, and I know that's no excuse, but I did it. And I got lucky, because nothing bad happened."

Peer pressure and just plain poor decision making are often the reasons that kids abuse prescription drugs. The reasons for popping pills often are little different from the reasons for smoking or drinking. People, adults as well as kids, want to feel a little different or feel a little better. Their friends are doing it, so why not? For a lot of kids, taking drugs is a way to show that they're grown up or that they can fit in. For others, it's a way of cutting loose and feeling good. Many young people have a difficult time thinking ahead and considering the consequences of their behavior. There often does not seem to be any price to pay for experimenting with drugs.

Prescription drugs are not as widely abused as other types of drugs, but they are often even more dangerous.

Prescription drug abuse is not as widespread as the abuse of drugs such as marijuana. However, a survey by the federal government in 1997 discovered that 6 percent of all high school tenth graders had abused tranquilizers at least once. That was roughly three times the number who had tried crack cocaine.

Someone who abuses prescription drugs often doesn't know what he or she is taking, let alone what the safe dose is. That's why prescription drug abuse can be more dangerous than smoking marijuana. A doctor's prescription for a painkiller may be very appropriate for a three-hundred-pound man laid up in bed

44 with torn ligaments. It could prove fatal for an eighty-pound young woman who has just had half a bottle of vodka.

Street or "home" versions of prescription medicines present another problem. These versions may contain impurities that multiply the drug's effects or side effects. The substances may not even be what the dealer says or thinks they are. There's no quality control in the black market.

A Serious Problem

Prescription drug abuse is a serious problem in the United States. Strategies for dealing with it vary, depending on the situation and the drug involved. Many programs, however, are similar to those used to combat other types of substance abuse.

If you suspect that you or someone you know has a problem, you should try to get help as soon as you can. Guidance departments and school nurses may offer help and advice. They often are in touch with local abuse-assistance programs. Other people to talk to include doctors, mental health organizations, religious leaders, and the police.

Some adults don't take prescription drug abuse as seriously as they do other forms of drug abuse. That can be a serious mistake. The DEA estimates that more than two million people a year use prescription drugs for nonmedical reasons.

From 1978 to 1984, Dana Plato entertained audiences as Kimberly Drummond on the television sitcom *Diff'rent Strokes.* Plato's career nosedived in the early 1990s, when she was arrested for robbing a video store in Las Vegas. The next year she was arrested for forging prescriptions for Valium.

Plato told the news media that she was lucky she had been caught. She had been abusing pills so badly, she said, that she had feared she would eventually die of an overdose.

Plato appeared to clean up her act. But rumors of drug abuse continued to dog her. In May 1999, she went on Howard Stern's radio program and told his audience that she was taking painkillers to cope with the pain from an extracted wisdom tooth. But that operation had taken place four months before.

A few days after the Stern broadcast, she died of an accidental overdose. Police said that the actress apparently had taken too much Valium and a hydrocodone painkiller before taking a nap. She fell asleep, never to wake up.

CHAPTER 6

Reactions and Interactions

Sally and Jim were out in the backyard doing some gardening. Suddenly Jim realized that Sally wasn't in the garden anymore. He called to her but didn't get an answer. Finally, he found her nearby sitting on the ground in the shade.

Sally's skin was whiter than a sheet of paper. She could barely talk. When he thought to check her pulse, he found it was very weak.

"I think it's just the infection," she said. Sally had been to the doctor earlier that day. She had been diagnosed with an internal infection and been given a prescription. "I think I'll be better after I take another pill. It's almost time," she mumbled.

"Maybe we should call the doctor instead," said Jim. Sally was so weak she didn't

argue, which convinced Jim that something must be wrong.

A Bad Reaction

Even when used correctly, prescription drugs can prove deadly. That's because they occasionally have unforeseen effects. People can experience allergic reactions to them. Or the drugs can interact with other substances that a patient is taking.

It turned out that Sally was having a reaction to the drug she was taking, perhaps because it was sulfur-based. She was allergic to anything containing sulfites, such as wine, although she didn't know it at the time. Her reaction was relatively easy to treat. All she had to do was stop taking the drug. Her doctor was able to give her a prescription for a different drug.

Most allergic reactions to drugs are even milder than Sally's. Antibiotics such as penicillin are among the most common drugs to which people are allergic. In most cases, the reaction is simply a rash or hives.

Still, doctors do not take reactions lightly. Although it is highly unlikely, severe cases can be life threatening. Health experts say that it is important to alert doctors, dentists, and pharmacists to any allergies that you know about. If, after taking a medicine, you

48 develop unusual or disturbing symptoms, you should immediately contact the physician who prescribed the drug.

Allergic reactions to drugs are only one potential problem. As drugs become more chemically complex, the ways in which they interact with other substances, especially other medicines, get more complicated. Pharmacists study these interactions. They often can head off trouble, but only if they know about all of the drugs that a patient is taking. That is why, even if you go to the same drugstore all the time, it is a good idea to discuss all of your medications—and the possible interactions with other drugs—whenever you get a new prescription. That includes over-the-counter drugs as well. Some medicines, such as cold remedies, may contain ingredients that will react with other prescription drugs.

The most dangerous interactions often come when a drug's beneficial effects are multiplied beyond what's intended. That multiplying factor is a special problem when drugs are abused, since there aren't any experts around to warn you of the dangers. Alcohol makes for an especially deadly mix. There have been numerous cases of people dying after mixing booze and barbiturates or similar pills. In effect,

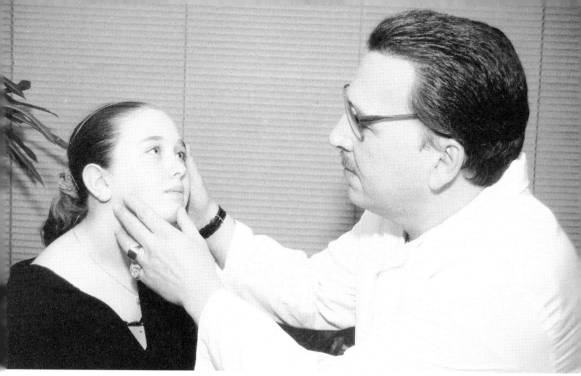

If you experience an unusual reaction to a prescription drug, see a doctor right away.

alcohol and drugs are a package plan for shutting down your body's vital functions.

Potential harmful reactions don't mean that you should be paranoid about taking medicine. They occur in a very small percentage of cases. But they do mean that you should be an informed patient. Your doctor and pharmacist usually know a great deal about the medicines you've been prescribed or want to buy. But you can also get information from publications such as *The Pill Book*, which is published by Bantam Books and is updated every few years. Information on different drugs also is available from Web sites, pharmaceutical companies, and drugstores. Beware of the

50 medical information you get from Web sites, however, unless they are sponsored by reputable medical organizations. In general, it's important to follow all directions that come with the medicine. Unless the instructions say otherwise, prescriptions should be taken until they are gone.

Always alert your doctor or your pharmacist if you experience a reaction to a drug, or even if you think you are experiencing a reaction. Never combine drugs without your doctor's knowledge. And above all, don't mix alcohol or illegal substances with prescription drugs.

CHAPTER 7

How Do You Tell Someone . . .

Clinton Middle School psychologist Stephanie Mars was counseling a student when she was startled by a knock on her door. The staff were under strict instructions never to interrupt her during a session unless there was an emergency. And the second Stephanie opened the door and saw the teacher's ashen face, she knew that this was one.

"They need you in the nurse's office," said the teacher.

Stephanie walked quickly down the hall, her footsteps echoing loudly. She reminded herself to be calm and tried to prepare herself for what she might find.

A lot of bad things ran through her head. So she was relieved when she found seventh grader

52 | *Scott Smith sitting in front of the nurse's desk. Then she saw how pale his face was and realized that he was having trouble breathing.*

"Scott?"

He started to say something to her, then bent forward and began throwing up.

"He took something from one of his friends," said the nurse, helping the seventh grader to the bathroom. "The principal is on the way."

Scott threw up again. He was hyperventilating and shaking. Was it panic? Or was it a drug overdose? Stephanie and the nurse couldn't be sure. They pushed a chair into the small lavatory and helped Scott sit down.

"Put your head between your legs," Stephanie told him. "Now breathe. Breathe very slowly. Very slowly."

"It was a caffeine pill," said Scott. "I got it from Jimmy Ziza."

"Just breathe," Stephanie repeated. As she held his head in her hands, she worried that he was going to die. She hoped that her fear was exaggerated. It had to be, she thought. A caffeine pill was harmless, wasn't it?

"His heart is racing," reported the nurse, checking his pulse. "I'm going to check his blood pressure. This is too strong a reaction for a caffeine pill."

Stephanie, on her knees next to Scott, agreed. "How many pills?" she asked.

"One," he said, gulping for air.

"Breathe," she told him. "But slowly. Deep breaths."

Scott leaned forward, his stomach heaving. Nothing came out. Stephanie squeezed his hand tightly.

"I'm sorry, Miss Mars," he said. Tears were in his eyes. "Am I going to die?"

"Just breathe, Scott," she said, as gently as she could. "It'll be all right."

He nodded, then put his head back between his legs. His breathing still wasn't normal, but it didn't seem quite so bad. Stephanie asked for more details about what he had taken.

"Did you see the box or bottle of pills?"

Scott shook his head no.

"How do you know it was caffeine?"

"Jimmy said."

Scott leaned forward and threw up again. The principal appeared behind Stephanie, asking what was going on. The nurse explained that Scott had felt his heart racing in class. As soon as he'd come into her office he felt very ill.

"He took a caffeine pill," the nurse said. "And he's having a bad reaction. But it can't be that serious. It's only caffeine."

"We can't be sure what he took," said Stephanie. As a school psychologist at Clinton, she often helped kids who had varied problems. She called them "her kids." Scott was a pretty

54 | *good student, better than average. He wasn't the most popular kid in the seventh grade, but he wasn't the most unpopular, either. He was just an ordinary kid who hadn't caused many problems. Until now.*

"We're going to have to get him to the hospital," Stephanie told the principal. "And we better find out if anyone else took these pills."

Jimmy Ziza and three other boys were soon sitting in the back of a police car, following the ambulance with Scott to St. Peter's Hospital. Jimmy swore that the pill he had given Scott was a caffeine pill. He had taken one himself. So had the other boys. Only Scott had had a bad reaction.

By the time he got to the hospital, Scott's pulse and blood pressure had returned to normal. He also had stopped throwing up. The doctor had him sit for a few hours and then released him to his parents. He wasn't exactly sure what had happened. Perhaps there had been a bad reaction, perhaps the pill hadn't been caffeine, or perhaps Scott had had a panic attack, an extreme reaction to a fearful situation.

Back at school, Stephanie worried about how to deal with the incident. The entire school was in a panic over it. The principal made an announcement over the loudspeaker, explaining exactly what had happened. A lot of kids seemed relieved when word came that Scott was okay.

But Stephanie was still worried. How many **55**
times had Scott, and everyone else in school,
heard about how dumb it was to take drugs?
How many times did a teacher or a guidance
counselor or a guest speaker say, "Don't take
something when you don't know what it is?"

"It's easy to tell kids not to do it," Stephanie
told her sister later. "But it's hard to say it in a
way that they'll pay attention to."

In the next few weeks, Stephanie and one
of the school guidance counselors discussed the
incident with students. They used role-playing
games to help kids get the message. Scott and
his friends returned to school. After an in-
house suspension, they talked about how dumb
they had been.

Still, Stephanie had questions. "How do you
reach everybody?" she wondered. "How do you
make people believe what you're telling them?
Maybe they've taken the drug before and noth-
ing happened. Maybe they're looking to be part
of the crowd or feel a little happy. How do you
tell them that the risk isn't worth the gain?"

You've Heard This Before, But . . .

You've probably heard before a lot of the
things that have been said in this book. The
truth is, it's not very complicated. Even
when used correctly, prescription drugs are
very powerful and must be respected. It's

56 just plain stupid to abuse them. And swallowing a pill when you don't know for sure what it is rates as a big-time gamble.

Doctors, pharmacists, drug companies, federal agencies, and other groups all have worked hard to make modern medicine safe. We know more about drugs today than we did at any time in our history. And thanks to the efforts of educators and counselors, the potential for abusing prescription drugs is decreasing.

But the problem can't be entirely solved by doctors or pharmacists, nor by teachers or the government. It comes down to you. What you choose to do with your body makes a great deal of difference to your friends and counselors such as Stephanie, to doctors and nurses and principals, to brothers and sisters and fathers and mothers.

But mostly to you.

Glossary

amphetamines A family of drugs that speed up the body's activities. Sometimes called "pep pills" or "uppers."

anabolic steroids Steroids that affect the body's growth. They are related to testosterone. Anabolic steroids have dangerous side effects.

antidepressants Drugs used by psychiatrists and psychologists to help people suffering from clinical depression. Sometimes called mood elevators.

barbiturates A family of sedatives. The name comes from barbital, which was invented in 1903.

benzodiazepines A family of minor tranquilizers that includes Ativan, Dalmane, Halcion, Valium, Serax, and Xanax. These drugs calm the body's nervous reactions.

ludes Slang term for methaqualone or quaalude. A sedative with very dangerous side effects. Methaqualone is no longer manufactured in the United States, but pills are available illegally from other countries.

minor tranquilizers Drugs that are prescribed to calm anxiety, as opposed to stronger tranquilizers that promote sleepiness or cause unconsciousness.

58

opiate/opioid family   Painkillers related chemically to opium. Opioids are made synthetically. Opiates come from the poppy plant.

over-the-counter drugs   Common medicines that can be bought without a prescription, like aspirin and cough medicine.

painkillers   Generic term for drugs used to relieve pain. Used properly, painkillers help patients to recover from surgery and injury.

prescription medicine   Drugs available only from a licensed pharmacist with a prescription or order from a doctor.

Ritalin   Methylphenidate hydrochloride, used to treat attention deficit disorder, or ADD.

Robo shots   Slang term for drinking large quantities of cold or cough medicines to get high.

roofies   Slang name for Rohypnol, a member of the benzodiazepine family. Some men have used the drug to rape women by rendering them semiconscious.

Rx   The symbol for prescriptions.

schedule of drugs   A federal list of drugs. The rules for prescriptions differ depending on which schedule the medicine is listed.

sedatives   Drugs that sedate or "knock out" a patient so that he or she doesn't feel anything during an operation. Sedatives also are prescribed to relieve anxiety or reduce the possibility of epileptic seizures.

sports enhancers   General term for a wide range of substances that supposedly will give athletes an edge. They range from steroids and "presteroids" (or "prohormones") to vitamins. Many claims for prohormones and supplements have not been backed by science.

supplements   Substances, such as vitamins, that are used to supplement the diet or otherwise aid the body. Many experts argue that some claims made for supplements are false or misleading.

Where to Go for Help

In the United States

American Council for Drug Education
164 West 74th Street
New York, NY 10023
(800) 488-DRUG
Web site: http://www.acde.org

National Clearinghouse for Alcohol and
   Drug Information
P.O. Box 2345
Rockville, MD 20847
English: (800) 729-6686
Spanish: (800) 487-4889
Web site: http://www.health.org

National Council on Alcoholism and Drug
   Dependence (NCADD)
12 West 21st Street
New York, NY 10010
(800) NCA-CALL
Web site: http://www.ncadd.org

60

National Institute on Drug Abuse
(800) 662-HELP
All calls made to NIDA's hotline are confidential.

Substance Abuse and Mental Health
    Services Administration
Web site: http://www.samhsa.gov

In Canada

Narcotics Anonymous
P.O. Box 7500, Station A
Toronto, ON M5W 1P9
(416) 691-9519

Youth Detox Program
Family Services of Greater Vancouver
504 Cassiar Street
Vancouver, BC V5K 4M9
(604) 299-1131

For Further Reading

Colvin, Rod. *Prescription Drug Abuse: The Hidden Epidemic.* Omaha, NE: Addicus Books, 1995.

Gorman, Jack M., M.D. *The Essential Guide to Psychiatric Drugs.* New York: St. Martin's Press, 1990.

Greenfield, Daniel P., and Ralph Slovenko. *Prescription Drug Abuse and Dependence: How Prescription Drug Abuse Contributes to the Drug Abuse Epidemic.* London: Charles C. Thomas Publisher, 1997.

Jaffe, Jerome H., ed. *Encyclopedia of Drugs and Alcohol.* New York: Macmillan Library Reference USA, 1995.

Kuhn, Cynthia, Scott Swartzwelder, and Wilkie Wilson. *Buzzed.* New York: W. W. Norton, 1998.

Liska, Ken. *The Pharmacist's Guide to the Most Misused and Abused Drugs in America.* New York: Collier Books, 1988.

Sanberg, Paul, and Michael Bunsey. *Prescription Narcotics: The Addictive Painkillers.* New York: Chelsea House, 1986.

Simpson, Carolyn. *Rx: Reading and Following the Directions for All Kinds of Medications.* New York: Rosen Publishing Group, 1994.

Index

A

addiction/addictiveness, 17, 18, 19, 22, 23, 24, 26, 29
American Medical Association, 40
amphetamines, 10, 19, 31–32
analgesics, 25
antibiotics, 17, 47
antidepressants, 30–31
antihistamines, 15, 33–34
appetite suppressants, 31
aspirin, 15, 16, 19, 22

B

barbiturates, 26, 28, 34, 41, 49
benzodiazepines, 28–29

C

caffeine/caffeine pills, 31, 51–55
chemical dependency, 9, 29
codeine, 19, 21, 22, 23, 25
cough/cold medicine, 15, 33–34, 48

D

Dalmane, 28
Darvon, 12, 25
date rape drugs, 27, 29
Demerol, 24
depressants, 24, 29, 33
doctors, 11, 12, 15, 16, 17, 19, 29, 31, 43, 44, 47, 49, 50, 56
Drug Enforcement Administration (DEA), 25, 45

E

Empirin, 19, 21, 22

F

Federal Drug Administration (FDA), 12, 31
following directions, importance of, 16, 50

G

GHB (gamma-hydroxybutyrate), 26–27

H
Halcion, 28
heroin,18, 24
hydrocodone, 25, 45

L
Lortab, 25

M
marijuana, 41, 43
McGwire, Mark, 38
methadone, 25
methaqualone/quaalude, 26
morphine, 19
"Mother's Little Helper," 10

N
narcotic analgesics, 23
National Institute for Drug
        Abuse, 39–40
Nembutal, 26

O
opiates/opioids, 22–25
overdoses, 24, 30, 45
over-the-counter drugs,
        12, 48
    abuse of, 15, 33–34
    examples of, 15, 31
    explanation of, 14–16

P
painkillers, 7, 12, 19, 22–25,
        43, 45
peer pressure, 42
Percodan, 24
pharmacists, 11, 12, 15, 16,
        17, 19–20, 21–22, 47,
        48, 49, 50, 56
Pill Book, The, 49
Plato, Dana, 45

prescription drugs, 6–8, 9, 12,
        14, 15, 55–56
    abuse of, 8, 10–11, 41–45
    alcohol and, 8, 24, 29, 30,
        34, 48–49, 50
    examples of, 12, 21–33, 36
    explanation of, 16–20
    reactions to, 9, 12, 46–50
    regulation/control of,
        17, 18
    street/"home" versions of,
        44
propoxyphene, 12
Prozac, 30–31

R
recreational drug use, 8
Ritalin, 32–33
Robo shots, 33–34
Rohypnol, 29

S
schedules of drugs, 18–19
Seconal, 26
sedatives, 25–27, 29, 30
Serax, 28
steroids, 35–40
stimulants, 31–33

T
tolerances, 24
tranquilizers, 27–29, 43
tricyclic antidepressants, 30
Tuinal, 26

V
Valium, 28, 45
Vicodin, 25

X
Xanax, 28

64

About the Author

Jeremy Roberts is the pen name of Jim DeFelice. Jim often uses this name when he writes for young readers, which he tries to do as much as he can. He has written books on extreme sports, as well as a number of books on various aspects of drug addiction. His books for adults include techno-thrillers and a historical trilogy. Jim lives with his wife and son in a haunted house in upstate New York.

Photo Credits

Cover shot and interior shots by Maura Boruchow except for pp. 18, 25, 27 © International Stock, p. 43 by Ira Fox and p. 49 by Brian Silak.

Layout

Laura Murawski